Employment Guide

for the

Recent Graduate

Your Skills and Education

Make 'em Pay within a Day

by

Andre Mayer

Executive Summary

"Employment Guide for the Recent Graduate" was written for anyone who is completing an educational program and is seeking their first professional job. The book covers all the usual material a job seeking skills book does. However the approach to writing resumes, finding and contacting potential employers, and practicing interview techniques is quite different and much simpler than what other books propose.

Another factor that makes this work stand out is the inclusion of a straight forward section on how to cope with rejection. There are also tips regarding available employer incentives for job seekers and information about post hire forms to complete.

Cover design by Frank Galasso

http://www.frankgalasso.com

Copyright © 2013

CONTENTS

Introduction

"Hi, I'm pleased to meet you. Tell me about yourself."

You'll hear those words many times as you progress with your job search. That's really what job hunting is all about. It's being able to tell prospective employers who you are and how you can help them meet their goals. From a very early age, people have been telling you that you were special. You are. Now you have to figure out what makes you different from the other people who apply for the jobs that you want. Not only that but you have to tell the prospective employers how that makes you the best person for their business.

You'll have plenty of opportunities to tell them about yourself. You'll use at least three approaches: written, verbal and electronic. Cover letters, applications, resumes and follow up letters will be written and may also be electronic. Cold calling, informational interviewing, employment interviews and follow up calls will test your verbal skills.

Yeah, I know you just went through all those academic trials and tribulations and now there are more tests. It doesn't seem right but its reality. Hey, you're a smart person. You bought this book so that you could get through the job hunting stage as quickly as possible. You're ready to give it one more hard push to make all that academic studying pay off.

My goal is to make this as easy a process as possible and move you to the next chapter in your life. Speaking of next chapters, let's move on.

Applications

Let's get started. The application phase of the job hunting preparation should only take about ***half an hour.***

On the next page is a standard application. They all contain about the same type of questions. You should know that applications are a screening tool. In times when there are a lot people looking for a lot fewer jobs, applications are often used to <u>screen out candidates</u>. To make things worse, the employer is asking all the questions. They are the casino and you are the victim, (ah, gambler). You have very little room to shine on an application.

Your goal here is to get past the first screening. There are a few things you can do to increase your odds of making the first cut. First, if the application is written, use perfect penmanship and spelling. You bet neatness counts. Second, make sure all your information is correct. I can help you help yourself here by having you complete the blank application on the next page. Complete it accurately and neatly. Keep it with you so you can copy it on a real application. This copying stuff reminds you of your school days, doesn't it? You don't want to be waiting for an interview and spend time agonizing about an employment date, supervisor's name, telephone number or address. It's much easier to pull out your copy and copy it. The same holds true for electronic applications.

A few tips: Read the whole application over before you start writing on it. This way you'll minimize silly errors like putting your city on the same line as your street address and leaving a blank space where the city should have gone. You'll also notice that they are looking for the most recent information first.

You can try to be that little white light in the darkness in the "Title and duties" section. If you've earned bragging rights in your past jobs, internships, volunteer or extracurricular activities, academics, sports, etc., the application is your first chance to use them. A job does not have to be a paid job for application purposes. Just be sure to note that it was a volunteer, internship or extracurricular experience. Try to summarize the duties with the most impressive ones first. You'd stated that you cooked for thirty people long before you mentioned that you washed the dishes (psst...don't even bring up the washing dishes stuff). Another tip is to simply write "See Resume" on the Education and Work Experience section of the application. This works if you have all your dates in order.

A big tip: Never say that you were fired or quit a job on the application!! Yeah, I know you have to be honest on an application or you could be fired if they find out. I want you to be honest, just smartly honest. When employers see "fired" or "quit" it sends up more red flags than a Mao Tse Tung parade. My advice is to respond to the question of reason for leaving with "to be discussed at interview". This eliminates the "game over" penalty and gives you a chance to explain the circumstances. Hey, even if you were at fault and really screwed up, you can claim inexperience and a great learning experience that made you a better person. Of course if you were justified in your actions you can state that too. My point is that by NOT screening yourself out, you have a fighting chance at the interview level.

Another big tip: Make sure you get permission from your references before you start using their name. This puts them on notice that they may be contacted regarding you and gives them time to think about you as a worker. There are also times when the person being asked to give a reference may like the job seeker in some ways but can't speak about their character as it pertains to the work environment. For example I knew a young lady who was very skilled in her work but was interested in a job located in a high crime area. I knew she had no idea about what she was getting into and I was very glad that she didn't ask me to be a reference for her.

A little tip: Social Security numbers are a necessary evil. You need to provide one so that a company can research your past. That's fair enough, but you don't need to share it with every employer you apply to. They already have your name, address, and telephone number. You don't want to be a victim of identity theft. I recommend that you write "**will provide at interview**" instead. This will at least limit the number of people who have this information.

Below is an example of a 2-page application. You can download a copy to practice on here: http://savoyinn.files.wordpress.com/2013/03/job-application.pdf

APPLICATION FOR EMPLOYMENT

PERSONAL INFORMATION

DATE OF APPLICATION:_____

Name: _____
               Last   First   Middle

Address: _____
          Street   (Apt)   City/State   Zip

Alternate Address: _____
                   Street   City/State   Zip

Contact Information: _____(____)_____(____)_____
                Home Telephone   Mobile Telephone   Email

How did you learn about our company?

POSITION SOUGHT: _____

Available Start Date:_____

Desired Pay Range: _____
               Hourly or Salary

Are you currently employed? _____

EDUCATION

	Name and Location	Graduate? – Degree?	Major / Subjects of Study
High School			
College or University			
Specialized Training, Trade School, etc...			
Other Education			

Please list your areas of highest proficiency, special skills or other items that may contribute to your abilities in performing the above mentioned position.

_____

_____

_____

PREVIOUS EXPERIENCE

Please list beginning from most recent

Dates Employed	Company Name	Location	Role/Title

Job notes, tasks performed and reason for leaving:

_____

_____

_____

_____

Dates Employed	Company Name	Location	Role/Title

Job notes, tasks performed and reason for leaving:

_____

_____

_____

_____

Dates Employed	Company Name	Location	Role/Title

Job notes, tasks performed and reason for leaving:

_____

_____

_____

_____

Dates Employed	Company Name	Location	Role/Title

Job notes, tasks performed and reason for leaving:

_____

_____

_____

Resumes

This is the longest and perhaps the hardest part of your job search preparation. This could take you up to *two and a half hours.*

Most Job Hunting books start this section by telling readers to make a list of their skills and abilities and to write down all the things they did on their jobs. Well, that makes sense and is probably a good way to do a future resume. I think it's much too hard an approach for your first resume. I'm going to show you some tricks later on but first a few rules.

Resumes are not in sentence form. They are in the past tense. They tell the employer what you want him or her to know about you. You are in charge here. Your goal is to put on paper what makes you special as a person, as a student and as a worker. You need to back up everything you write on a resume with facts...either on the resume or in the interview.

Ok, let's get started.

As this book is geared towards recent graduates of a skills training program, I'm going to help you create a **student resume**. First type your name in larger than average font. Now make it bold and in the center of the page. The next line is your address. Next include your telephone number and an alternate number. Under this, put your email address (a professional looking e-mail address, NOT sexxydog@gmail.com). All right, the heading is done. Look at you all proud of yourself smiling away. It's going to get better. Let's go.

The easiest way to show you how to write a resume is by using the "Show and Tell" method (Ah yes, kindergarten all over again). So, I'm going to introduce you to four recent graduates from different educational backgrounds. Hopefully one of these people will be someone you can relate to.

First I'll introduce you to Roberto who just completed a ten week training course in culinary arts where he learned the basics of kitchen sanitation, cooking and baking. He has some related experience as a Prep Cook and a Dishwasher.

Roberto wants to tell his next boss what skills he has for him or her to utilize in the work environment. But what would his boss be looking for? He doesn't even know this person. Not to fear, our first electronic cheat sheet is near. Sounding more and more like school isn't it?

Roberto wants to know more about what skills are needed in the cooking business. So, he goes to **O*NET OnLine** now in a free easily available electronic format at http://www.onetonline.org, he scrolls down to "Occupational Search", types in "Cook", selects "go", and scrolls down and selects "Cooks and Food preparation workers". As he reads the whole segment, he can easily find other skills not listed just in the "Other qualifications" section.   For now he focuses on the "Other qualifications"section. Here he finds out what the bosses are looking for. The **O*NET OnLine** says cooks have the following: "***Other qualifications.*** Cooks and food preparation workers must be efficient, quick, and work well as part of a team. Manual dexterity is helpful for cutting, chopping, and plating. These workers also need creativity and a keen sense of taste and smell. Personal cleanliness is essential because most States require health certificates indicating that workers are free from communicable diseases. Knowledge of a foreign language can be an asset because it may improve communication with other restaurant staff, vendors, and the restaurant's clientele." (Underline added).

Now all he has to do is select the skills that match both him and the job. He doesn't want to **be greedy here. If he doesn't possess a skill listed then he doesn't state it.** If he doesn't have a sense of smell, he should not claim to have one. He can however add to the list if he feels it may be a benefit to an employer. Roberto included in his resume that he was motivated to finish tasks. He correctly thinks that an employer would like this quality in Roberto. So far, here's what we have.

Roberto Perez

1098 North Street
Providence , RI 02903

(401) 725-1010 Home
(401) 678-1234 Cell
Robperez@yahoo.com

Skills

Efficient, quick worker	Good manual dexterity
Excellent hygiene	Good sense of smell and taste
Safety conscious	Ability to finish tasks
Bi-lingual Spanish	Good people skills

Now, Roberto earned a credential that makes him stand out from the pack, this is where he wants to show it off. Roberto is ServSafe certified which puts him a step ahead of the other culinary candidates. His bragging rights are as follows:

Credentials

Servsafe certified in April, 2010

Roberto completed a certificate program where he learned cooking skills and received his ServSafe certification. His education section describes what he learned in order of importance and logical chronology. He puts the most job relevant education first. His education section looks like this:

Education

<u>**Outstanding Culinary Arts School**</u>, April, 2010

Servsafe curriculum, knife skills, basic cooking, basic baking, measuring, time management, reading catering orders, filling catering orders.

<u>**Smarty Pants High School**</u>, Providence, Rhode Island, June 2008.

Roberto was a prep cook and a dishwasher before that. He looked up "prep cook" in the **Dictionary of Occupational Titles** via http://www.occupationalinfo.org and found the following:

TITLE(s): **COOK HELPER (hotel & rest.)**

Assists workers engaged in preparing foods for hotels, restaurants, or ready-to-serve packages by performing any combination of following duties: Washes, peels, cuts, and seeds vegetables and fruits. <u>Cleans, cuts, and grinds meats, poultry,</u> and seafood. <u>Dips food items in crumbs, flour, and batter to bread them.</u> Stirs and strains soups and sauces. <u>Weighs and measures designated ingredients.</u> Carries pans, kettles, and trays of food to and from work stations, stove, and refrigerator. *Stores foods in designated areas, utilizing knowledge of temperature requirements and food spoilage.* Cleans work areas, equipment and utensils, segregates and removes garbage and steam-cleans or hoses garbage containers. (Underline added).

In the example below, you can see that Roberto picked and chose the parts of the job that were most impressive. He left out things like "Carries pans, kettles, and trays of food to and from work stations, stove, and refrigerator" because that in itself doesn't add much value to his skill set. He also omitted the cleaning and washing parts of the job as he will cover that in the "Dishwasher" job he had held. He added "Made corn bread. Cooked vegetables to order" because these were impressive things he did at Boston Market but weren't listed in the above description of a Cooks Helper.

Roberto's previous job was dishwasher. He looked at both the descriptions in the **Dictionary of Occupational Titles** and the "**O*Net OnLine**". He chose the latter description as it seemed to represent the actual tasks that he performed without stating the needless minutia.

--Wash dishes, glassware, flatware, pots, and/or pans using dishwashers or by hand.

--Place clean dishes, utensils, and cooking equipment in storage areas.

--Maintain kitchen work areas, equipment, and utensils in clean and orderly condition.

--Stock supplies such as food and utensils in serving stations, cupboards, refrigerators, and salad bars.

--Sweep and scrub floors.

--Clean garbage cans with water or steam.

--Sort and remove trash, placing it in designated pickup areas.

--Clean and prepare various foods for cooking or serving.

--Set up banquet tables.

--Transfer supplies and equipment between storage and work areas, by hand or using hand trucks.

This is how Roberto put his culinary experience together on his resume. He simply chose the "template" from the electronic media, copied and pasted the tasks that applied to him, and **changed the tense to past tense for resume format.**

Culinary Experience

Prep Cook, The Great Restaurant, Providence, Rhode Island (2007 -2008)

Cleaned, cut, and grinded meats and poultry. Dipped food items in crumbs, flour, and batter to bread them. Weighed and measured designated ingredients. Stored foods in designated areas, utilizing knowledge of temperature requirements and food spoilage. Made corn bread. Cooked vegetables to order.

Dishwasher, Stinky's Restaurant, Clarksville, Tennessee (2004-2005)

Washed dishes, glassware, flatware, pots, and/or pans using dishwashers and by hand. Placed clean dishes, utensils, and cooking equipment in storage areas. Maintained kitchen work areas, equipment, and utensils in clean and orderly condition. Stocked supplies such as food and utensils in serving stations, cupboards, refrigerators, and salad bars.

Let's see what the whole enchilada looks like.

Roberto Perez

1098 North Street
Providence , RI 02903
(401) 725-1010 Home, (401) 678-1234 Cell
Robperez@yahoo.com

Skills

Efficient, quick worker

Excellent hygiene

Safety conscious

Bi-lingual Spanish

Good manual dexterity

Good sense of smell and taste

Ability to finish tasks

Good people skills

Credentials

Servsafe certified in April, 2010

Education

Outstanding Culinary Arts School, April, 2010

Servsafe curriculum, knife skills, basic cooking, basic baking, measuring, time management, reading catering orders, filling catering orders.

Smarty Pants High School, Providence, Rhode Island, June 2008

Culinary Experience

Prep Cook, The Great Restaurant, Providence, Rhode Island (2007 -2008)

Cleaned, cut, and grinded meats and poultry. Dipped food items in crumbs, flour, and batter to bread them. Weighed and measured designated ingredients. Stored foods in designated areas, utilizing knowledge of temperature requirements and food spoilage. Made corn bread. Cooked vegetables to order.

Dishwasher, Stinky's Restaurant, Clarksville, Tennessee (2004-2005)

Washed dishes, glassware, flatware, pots, and/or pans using dishwashers and by hand. Placed clean dishes, utensils, and cooking equipment in storage areas. Maintained kitchen work areas, equipment, and utensils in clean and orderly condition. Stocked supplies such as food and utensils in serving stations, cupboards, refrigerators, and salad bars.

Impressive so far, wouldn't you say? Now let's try another resume example.

Mary completed an A.S. degree in accounting at a community college and is starting her resume. Again she goes to the trusty **O*NET OnLine** and reads the article. The "Work environment" section gives her some clues as to what employers might be looking for.

"Work environment. Bookkeeping, accounting, and auditing clerks work in an <u>office environment</u>. They may experience <u>eye and muscle strain, backaches, headaches, and repetitive motion injuries from using computers on a daily basis. Clerks may have to sit for extended periods while reviewing detailed data."</u>

Many bookkeeping, accounting, and auditing clerks work regular business hours and a standard 40-hour week, although some may work <u>occasional evenings and weekends.</u> About 1 out of 4 clerks worked part time in 2008.

Bookkeeping, accounting, and auditing clerks <u>may work longer hours to meet deadlines</u> at the end of the fiscal year, during tax time, or when monthly or yearly accounting audits are performed. Additionally, those who work in hotels, restaurants, and stores may put in overtime during peak holiday and vacation seasons." (Underline added)

Here are her clues. "Office environment" means working well with others. Potential physical ailments can be overcome by having an active "off work" schedule and rest. "May work longer hours to meet deadlines" means you have to be goal oriented. Of course you should include the obvious like good math skills.

So now she has:

Mary Cartier

1098 South Street
Providence, RI 02903

(401) 333-1110 Home
(401) 135-1234 Cell
Mcartier@gmail.com

Skills

Detail oriented worker	Good vision
Good math skills	Health conscious
Ability to finish tasks	People skills
Conscientious	Bi-lingual French

Ok, you get the idea. Isn't the **O*NET OnLine** a great tool? We'll be using it again later. Wait till you see the **Dictionary of Occupational Titles**!

Mary won an accounting scholarship. She lets the potential bosses know about her accomplishment like this:

Awards

College Accounting Scholarship Merit recipient, 2010

Now we move to the meat of her resume... her education.

Mary graduated from a Community College with a major in Accounting. She wants to show off her great grades and what she learned in accounting. Problem is that her overall average was a 2.7 out of a 4.0. Look how she got around this problem and was able to show off her academic skills. She also highlighted her most advanced coursework under a "Relevant Coursework" section.

Education

A.S. Computational Community College, Providence, Rhode Island. Major G.P.A. = 3.75

Relevant Coursework

Financial Accounting   Intermediate Accounting 1 and 2
Managerial Accounting   Computerized Accounting
Personal Income Taxes   Personal Finance

The next section includes Employment experience. She can include her volunteer or internship experience here. She wants to show off her Related Experience before any other non-related jobs she's had. Here she has several opportunities to borrow from her two newest best friends, The **Dictionary of Occupational Titles** and the "**O*NET OnLine**".

The first approach is to look up the job titles that she's had in the past and use the information to build her resume by "using" the skills and descriptions that fit her specific job.

Another strong suggestion is to **also look up the title of the job she is now applying for and point out and emphasize the skills and abilities she possesses which are needed in the new job.**

Mary worked as a bookkeeper for several years before acquiring formal training. She did a lot of number crunching but can't find a way to intelligently put it on paper. So she goes to our newest best friend the **Dictionary of Occupational Titles** at http://www.occupationalinfo.org (DOT) and looks at the job tasks of a bookkeeper. Here she reads:

TITLE(s): **BOOKKEEPER (clerical)**

Keeps records of financial transactions for establishment, using calculator and computer: Verifies, allocates, and posts details of business transactions to subsidiary accounts in journals or computer files from documents, such as sales slips, invoices, receipts, check stubs, and computer printouts. Summarizes details in separate ledgers or computer files and transfers data to general ledger, using calculator or computer. Reconciles and balances accounts.

Mary also chose to "borrow" material from the http://www.onetonline.org (**O*Net OnLine**)

Tasks

- Operate computers programmed with accounting software to record, store, and analyze information.
- Check figures, postings, and documents for correct entry, mathematical accuracy, and proper codes.
- Classify, record, and summarize numerical and financial data to compile and keep financial records, using journals and ledgers or computers.
- Debit, credit, and total accounts on computer spreadsheets and databases, using specialized accounting software.
- Operate 10-key calculators, typewriters, and copy machines to perform calculations and produce documents.
- Receive, record, and bank cash, checks, and vouchers.
- Comply with federal, state, and company policies, procedures, and regulations.
- Compile statistical, financial, accounting or auditing reports and tables pertaining to such matters as cash receipts, expenditures, accounts payable and receivable, and profits and losses.
- Code documents according to company procedures.
- Reconcile or note and report discrepancies found in records.

(Underline added)

She can now pick and choose the actual tasks she performed and eliminate the rest (I did this for her by underlining the duties she actually performed). She was never responsible for complying with federal, state, and company policies, procedures, and regulations or complying with federal, state, and company policies, procedures, and regulations. That was her boss's job. The other two tasks: Operate computers programmed with accounting software to record, store, and analyze information; and Operate 10-key calculators, typewriters, and copy machines to perform calculations and produce documents were obvious and not worth mentioning .

She could pick and choose the best language from either of these resources. She wants to put the most impressive tasks first. She also doesn't want to be repetitive when using two sources. Mary also decided to "edit" the sources to make her resume flow smoother.

It's a lot easier than starting with a blank page, isn't it?

Her work experience is as follows.

Related Experience

Bookkeeper, Big Bucks Inc., 123 Cash Lane, Moneyville, MA 2007 to 2010

Verified, allocated, and posted details of business transactions to subsidiary accounts in computer files. Compiled accounting reports and tables pertaining to receipts, expenditures, accounts payable and receivable, and profits and losses. Reconciled and balanced accounts and transferred data to general ledger.

Mary primarily used the http://www.occupationalinfo.org (DOT) and added to it by using a task from http://www.onetonline.org (**O*Net OnLine**). Let's put these two student resumes together and see how they look.

(A little tip: As with the application, her "Related Experience" or your "Work Experience" doesn't have to be paid experience. She can certainly include internships and volunteer experiences on her resume.)

Let's see what this "Balance Sheet" or in her case "Statement of Employability Position" looks like.

Mary Cartier

1098 South Street
Providence, RI 02903
(401) 333-1110 Home, (401) 135-1234 Cell
Marycartier@gmail.com

Skills

Detail oriented worker
Good math skills
Ability to finish tasks
Conscientious

Good vision
Health conscious
People skills
Bi-lingual French

Awards

College Accounting Scholarship merit recipient, 2010

Education

A.S. Computational Community College, Providence, Rhode Island. Major G.P.A. = 3.75

Relevant Coursework

Financial Accounting
Managerial Accounting

Intermediate Accounting 1and 2
Computerized Accounting

Related Experience

Bookkeeper, Big Bucks Inc., 123 Cash Lane, Moneyville, MA 2007 to 2010

Verified, allocated, and posted details of business transactions to subsidiary accounts in computer files. Compiled accounting reports and tables pertaining to receipts, expenditures, accounts payable and receivable, and profits and losses. Reconciled and balanced accounts and transferred data to general ledger.

Other Work Experience

Life Guard, YMCA, 756 Wet Street, Lakeville, MA, 2006 to 2007

Monitored activities in swimming areas. Cautioned swimmers regarding unsafe areas. Rescued swimmers in danger of drowning and administered first aid.

As you see above, you can include other work experience even if it's not related to your goal. You could simply call it "Work Experience".

Remember that neatness, spacing, spelling and honesty are all important. When you state that you are a quick efficient worker, you should have a real life story or two explaining why that's a fact.

It's often said that resumes should be one page long. That's often the case and should be with yours as you are just starting out. However, once you build an impressive work and educational history, you'll want to let employers know about it... especially as your skill base grows. Remember that a tight concise Resume is better than a long repetitive one.

As your career progresses, you will no longer need the student resume. You will advance to using a chronological, functional, or analytical style. You will still be visiting your two friends, the **O*NET OnLine** and the "**Dictionary of Occupational Titles**". What you are learning here will be with you always.

A small note here. There wasn't enough room on the page for a "References" section, so I eliminated it. "References" listed on a resume is the least important section as it usually says nothing about you.

A little typing trick. After typing in a major category like "Education" or "Related Work Experience", I change my font size back to normal BEFORE hitting the enter key. This keeps my spacing small and consistent. So, if "Education" is in 14 font, I change the font to 12 before I hit enter.

E-mail tricks. When E-mailing a resume to an employer, don't attach your resume. Include it in the body of the e-mail after the cover letter (see next section for cover letters). Some employers scan your resume for key words. If you effectively utilize your two best new friends (**O*Net OnLine** and DOT), you will pass both the screening test and the human test.

Let's look at two more student examples.

Thomas Tenspeed attended a technical school and learned marine mechanics. He wants to showcase his skills and abilities as they relate to his future job. So he went online and searched the **O*Net OnLine** and found marine mechanic. Reading through the "Knowledge and Skills" sections he noticed **"Customer and Personal Service** — Knowledge of principles and processes for providing customer and personal services. This includes customer needs assessment, meeting quality standards for services, and evaluation of customer satisfaction" and **"Active Listening** — Giving full attention to what other people are saying, taking time to understand the points being made, asking questions as appropriate, and not interrupting at inappropriate times." Tom has always been a good listener and is easy to get along with. These are skills that other people trained in the same profession may not have. That might be the difference between him and another candidate for a job. He lists **"Excellent Listening and Communication"** as his first skill.

As a marine mechanic he has to be mechanically inclined. He had taken a pre-test to assess his natural abilities in the mechanical field and scored in the top 10% of all people taking the test. He was also a good student in the class. The **O*Net OnLine** lists four items in the "Knowledge" section. Three of them are in the mechanical area the other is in customer service. Tom puts **"Innate and learned Mechanical skills"** as his second skill. He can bring a copy of the pre-test and his grades to an interview to verify his assertions.

Reading further into the **O*Net OnLine's** description of marine mechanic he notices **"Troubleshooting"** as a skill requirement for the job. From his experiences at school and from his previous employment as a bicycle repairer he knows how important this is to an employer. Finding and fixing the problem the first time is how a mechanic builds a good reputation and how the employer develops loyal customers. Turns out that Tom is very good at this. So he lists it as his third skill. Thomas continues to find other skills that are important for a marine mechanic to have that he indeed does possess and lists them too.

Thomas begins his resume like this:

Thomas Tenspeed

26 Spoke Lane
Schwinnville, Ohio 66666
708-555-1111

Skills

Excellent listening and communication

Innate and learned mechanical skills

Troubleshooting

Problem solving

Deductive reasoning

Good vision and hearing

Tom now turns to the Education section of his resume. He lists the school he attended and the **most relevant** courses to the job he will be doing. He gets this information from his school's course catalog.

Marine Technical Institute, 1234 Fall River Avenue, Seekonk MA

Marine Mechanic courses included:

Outboard engines

Two- and four-stroke engines

Electrical systems

Stern drive engines

Fuel systems

Hull design

He then moves on to show his "mechanical" related experience. Since he is going to describe the tasks that he completed as a bicycle repairer, he thought that using the **Dictionary of Occupational Titles** would be the best way to select the job duties that pertained to him. He found "Bicycle repairer" in the DOT and printed it out. He also looked up "Bicycle repairer" in the **O*Net OnLine** and printed that out as well.

Comparing the two descriptions, he liked the way the "**O*Net OnLine**" listed the tasks better than the **Dictionary of Occupational Title's** approach. Tom didn't like the ranking of tasks though; so he rearranged them in the order in which he felt the most impressive duties stood out. For example, Tom felt that welding bicycle frames was more important than assembling bikes so he changed the order.

Now Tom has his related experience as follows:

Bicycle Repairer, Schulz's Schwinn Shop, 4-10-09 to 9-1-09
- Welded broken or cracked frames together, using oxyacetylene torches and welding rods.
- Shaped replacement parts, using bench grinders.
- Disassembled axles in order to repair, adjust, and replace defective parts, using hand tools.
- Installed and adjusted speed and gear mechanisms.
- Assembled new bicycles.

Let's see how Tom's resume looks now that he's built it.

Thomas Tenspeed

26 Spoke Lane
Schwinnville, Ohio 66666
708-555-1111

Skills

Excellent listening and communication

Innate and learned mechanical skills

Troubleshooting

Problem solving

Deductive reasoning

Good vision and hearing

Education

Marine Technical Institute, 1234 Fall River Avenue, Seekonk MA

Marine Mechanic courses included:

Outboard engines

Two- and four-stroke engines

Electrical systems

Stern drive engines

Fuel systems

Hull design

Related Work Experience

Bicycle Repairer, Schulz's Schwinn Shop, 4-10-09 to 9-1-09

- Welded broken or cracked frames together, using oxyacetylene torches and welding rods.
- Shaped replacement parts, using bench grinders.
- Disassembled axles in order to repair, adjust, and replace defective parts, using hand tools.
- Installed and adjusted speed and gear mechanisms.
- Assembled new bicycles.

While doing this exercise, Tom became more confident in himself and his ability to interview effectively for a marine mechanic job. By researching the marine mechanic and the bicycle repairer positions in the **O*Net OnLine** and the DOT, he was able to see a lot of overlap of skills and abilities. He knew he was heading in the right direction for his life. Seeing that his skills, knowledge, and abilities fit very well with his goals puts him in a great pre-interview state of mind. He is now self confident and eager to tell employers what he can do for them.

One point of correction on Tom's resume. He doesn't have an e-mail address for employers to contact him at. In today's world it looks as if Tom is out of touch with the times. Don't be that guy!

Let's look at one more recent graduate.

Nancy Nunes just graduated from a four year college in nursing. Along the way, she worked as a Nurse Assistant and also completed her internship as a Student Nurse. We'll start our research part of her resume with http://www.onetonline.org to find the skills that potential employers are looking for. Then we'll use http://www.occupationalinfo.org" to help us write the Related Experience section of her resume. As you already know how and where to find the information, I'm just going to put it together. You should go back to the sources to see what I borrowed from them. If you cut and paste material, you may want to re-type it as the font may not be the same...even if you "doctor" it.

Here we go.

Nancy Nunes

247 Health Street
Boston, MA 01019

(508) 777-8975 or (508) 675-2364
Nnunes@mail.com

Skills

Caring and empathetic

Emotionally strong

Athletic and physically strong

Bi-lingual Portuguese

Detail oriented

Educationally oriented

Great interpersonal skills

Team player

Credentials

Registered Nurse, Bachelor's degree, Massachusetts, 2010
National Student Nurses Association member, 2008 to 2010

Education

B.S. University of Massachusetts, Amherst, MA 01003- 9299. Major G.P.A. = 3.80

Relevant Coursework

Nursing Care of Adults: Acute

Nursing Care of Adults: Chronic

Pharmacology in Nursing

Psychiatric-Mental Health Nursing

Related Experience

Clinical Experience, University of Massachusetts Medical Center, 55 North Lake Avenue, Worcester, MA 01655-0002

Nurse Assistant, Saint Vincent Hospital, 123 Summer Street, Worcester, MA 01608, 2007 to 2010.

Took and recorded temperature, blood pressure, pulse and respiration rates, and food and fluid intake and output. Cleaned, sterilized, stored, prepared, and issued dressing packs, treatment trays, and other supplies. Turned and repositioned bedfast patients, alone or with assistance, to prevent bedsores.

Cover Letters

Now that your resume is finished, you're about half done with the job hunt preparation. Revising the cover letters that I give you to meet your needs shouldn't take more than ***half an hour.***

Cover Letters are a formal method of introducing yourself and your resume to your prospective boss. Cover letters are used when you are responding to a job posting from a newspaper or an online site. Your cover letter should tell the employer how you heard about the opportunity and then go right into telling them what makes you special. Next, ask for an interview. Make sure you include a resume.

Roberto Perez
1098 North Street
Providence, RI 02903

3/2/2010

Mr. John Smith
Freddy's Foods
22 Hungry Street
Cranston, RI

Dear Mr. Smith,

I am applying for the food service position advertised in the Providence Journal on 3/1/2010. I recently completed a culinary arts program and am Servsafe certified. I have enclosed a copy of my resume for your review.

My strengths include being a safe worker, great eye-hand coordination, time management skills, interpersonal skills and speed.

Please contact me at your earliest convenience to schedule an interview.

I am eager to discuss this position with you or your staff.

Sincerely,

Roberto Perez

Enclosure: Resume

Here's an example of a cover letter for Mary Cartier

Mary Cartier
1098 South Street
Providence, RI 02903

3/2/2010

Mr. Alfred Numbersmith
Al's Accounting
22 Count Street
Providence, RI

Dear Mr. Numbersmith,

I am applying for the Junior Accountant position advertised in the Providence Journal on 3/1/2010. I recently completed an A.S. degree from Computational Community College in Providence, Rhode Island. I'm proud to say that my major G.P.A. was 3.75. I'm equally proud of having won a College Accounting Scholarship in 2010.

I have enclosed a copy of my resume for your review.

My strengths include being a detail oriented, focused, and productive worker. I also possess a pleasant personality and am easy to get along with.

Please contact me at your earliest convenience to schedule an interview.

I am eager to discuss this position with you or your staff.

Sincerely,

Mary Cartier

Enclosure: Resume

You can see that Mary immediately flashes out her strong points right at the beginning of the cover letter. This captures the employer's attention. She also knows that employers are looking for two things: someone who can do the job and someone they can get along with. She lets her prospective employer know from the beginning that she is a congenial person.

Nancy Nunes
247 Health Street
Boston, MA 01019

3/2/2010

Ms. Holly Health
Good Medicine Hospital
875 Wellness Street
Providence, RI

Dear Ms. Health,

I am applying for the Registered Nurse position advertised in the Providence Journal on 3/1/2010. I recently completed a B.S. degree from the University of Massachusetts at Amherst, MA where I earned a G.P.A. of 3.80 in my major.

I have enclosed a copy of my resume for your review.

My strengths include being dedicated to the field of nursing. I am technically strong as my course records indicate and have an innate ability to communicate well with patients, co-workers, and those in authority.

Please contact me at your earliest convenience to schedule an interview.

I am eager to discuss this position with you or your staff.

Sincerely,

Nancy Nunes

Enclosure: Resume

Another approach to a good cover letter is to take the requirements of the ad and indicate how you fit each of those requirements. I like this approach for people who have been in the work force for some time. You're just starting out so I recommend keeping it short and simple.

Where the Jobs Are

Here we are only four hours into the job search preparation and you're ready to start identifying potential employers. Believe it or not, this step should only take you *half an hour* to complete.

Now that you have a cover letter and a resume you are ready to start looking for a job! Where do you look?

The obvious answer is with your school's placement program. They may be able to assist you with referrals and leads. They may even teach you how to fine tune your resume and cover letter to expand upon what your skills are and more closely match what is required in your particular field. They may make connections with alumni who might want to meet bright recent grads such as you.

The Department of Labor has a "Job Bank, Career Center" in every state. To find the one closest to you, go to "www.careeronestop.org". On the right side of the page select your state name on the drop down menu. Here you will find resources like online job postings, copy machines and telephones for job seekers. It can be your home office away from home until you find a job. While you are here (or from your home) you could search for jobs by utilizing online web sites and respond with an electronic version of your cover letter and resume. Examples of online web sites would be: www.Hotjobs.yahoo.com, www.Monster.com, www.careerbuilder.com, www.craigslist.com, etc.

Another option would be the "Help Wanted Ads" in the local newspaper. The Sunday paper is the best "day" paper to use as it has more opportunities than any other day. Along the same line, you could respond to opportunities in trade journals in your field.

To reply, you send a cover letter and a resume to the name and address listed.

The problem with all these approaches is that you are competing with everyone who sees or hears about the opportunity. That could include people whose experience and abilities far exceed yours (for now).

The other problem is that you are now playing the waiting game. You're sitting by the phone waiting for someone to call. If you're somewhat proactive, you should be following up on potential jobs where you have sent resumes.

Don't get me wrong. I'm not discouraging you from doing this. You should apply to every job that remotely fits your expertise. However, I think you should be more proactive about your career.

First, go through each and every page of the local yellow pages in the area where you want to work and look at the captions. As you do so, ask yourself if there is any chance that people in that field might hire someone with your recently acquired skills. You may be surprised at how many employers might hire someone like you. Write down the categories and the alternate name of the category if any. You can find alternate names of categories in the index. For example if you want to be an aerobics instructor you may be referred to "Exercise and Physical Fitness Programs" and "Health Clubs & Gymnasiums". You could get the telephone numbers of each potential employer right from the low tech yellow pages.

Most people want to work as close to home as possible. So, to solve the problem of where the jobs are in the local area, we go to the internet.

We search for "Maps". I'm going to use "Mapquest" as I am most familiar with it but feel free to try other map sites as well. Once on your site, click on "Maps". Then type in **your address**. Next, near the top of your screen the site states "Find a Business *(optional)*" or "Search Nearby". In this section type in any of the categories you found in the yellow pages. Then hit enter and out of cyber space, there may appear dozens of companies that hire people just like you.

Depending on your career choice and where you live, you may find one source (Yellow pages or internet) better than the other. What really matters is that you have names of companies and telephone numbers with which you can start your job search.

Let's see how Roberto, Thomas, Mary and Nancy did on this exercise.

Roberto found 25 categories where there may be cooking jobs available. He selected his top 10 choices. They are:

Assisted Living	Meal Preparation services
Bakeries	Nursing Homes
Banquet Facilities	Pizza
Catering	Restaurants
Hotels	Hospitals

Thomas found only nine categories that were related to his newly acquired skills. They are:

Marinas	Boat Yards
Boat Builders	Boat Dealers
Boat Maintenance	Boat Repairing
Boat Equipment & Supplies	Marine Contractors
Marine Equipment & Supplies	

He was concerned that he hadn't found enough categories so he went back to **www.onetonline.org** and saw that **Outdoor Power Equipment and Other Small Engine Mechanics was a related job category that he could research if necessary.**

Mary found 32 categories that were directly related to accounting. Actually Mary picked a great field because most small companies and all medium to large companies have accounting departments. She focused on these 8:

Accountants   Banks
Credit Unions   Insurance companies
Credit and debt counseling services   Mortgages
Mutual Funds   Tax preparation services

Nancy chose:

Adult Care Facilities   Employee Assistance Programs
Drug Abuse and & addiction   Group Homes
Hospitals   Physicians
Medical Testing services   Nurse

By using both the Yellow pages and the internet you should be able to list about 10 employers per category. That's 100 employers to call on. That's not including the personal referrals from the professional you are meeting. Here's an example of what Thomas found on www.mapquest.com by simply entering "Marina" where MapQuest asks you if you want to "Search Nearby". Then he sorted by **distance** from his home.

Indian Pointe Marina   Pete's Boat Yard
13 Baywood Ave   725 Indiana St
Providence, RI   Warwick, RI
(401) 555-0001   (401) 555-0002

Clamshell Marina Inc   Port Hedgehog
1328 Aqua St   1128 Beer Blvd
East Providence, RI   Cranston, RI
(401) 555-0003   (401) 555-0004

Kevin's Marina Inc   Atlantic Marine Surveyors
81 County Rd   10 Shore Dr
Barrington, RI   Barrington, RI
(401) 555-0005   (401) 555-0006

Call on? Did you say call on? Yes I did. I told you I had a proactive approach to finding work.

The goal is to meet the people who have the power to hire you or at least teach you something and /or refer you to another potential employer. The first thing you have to do is find out who is the right person to talk to.

Now you need to take this list and start calling the people who would **SUPERVISE** you if you worked with them. You can find out who that is by calling the company and asking to speak to the head chef, manager, the chief accountant, the head nurse, etc. Your goal here is to get to meet this person whether they have an opening or not. You're looking for professional information and assistance in your career search. This is really what networking is all about. You get to meet the boss when there is no pressure on either of you. You're hoping to learn and to get a referral to someone else who might also be able to help you. **This is how 80% of all jobs are found.**

Once you have the correct contact name and title you should send a letter of introduction like Roberto and Nancy did. You can modify your initial "respond to an ad" cover letter quite simply.

Making Contacts

Now that you've identified your next potential employers, you need to contact them by mail, e-mail or telephone. The approach that works best is the one that you feel most comfortable with. I personally like the direct personal contact on the telephone. This may not be appropriate in all fields of employment due to the corporate structure. By modifying my sample letters or my "cold call script" you should have at least one or two interviews lined up in about *an hour of actual work time*.

Sample Cold Call Cover Letter

Roberto Perez
1098 North Street
Providence, RI 02903

3/2/2010

Mr. Robert Rotunda
Blakes Restaurant
22 Satisfaction Street
Pawtucket, RI

Dear Mr. Rotunda,

I would like to meet with you for some professional advice on how to find employment in my field.

I am a recent graduate of a culinary arts school and am Servsafe certified.

My strengths include being a safe worker, great eye-hand coordination, time management skills, interpersonal skills and speed.

I have attached a resume for your review. I hope that taking time to meet with me (about ten to fifteen minutes) is acceptable to you. I admire your success in your field and am eager to learn from you.

I will contact you later this week to schedule a convenient time for us to meet.

Thank you in advance for your consideration.

Sincerely,

Roberto Perez

Nancy Nunes
247 Health Street
Boston, MA 01019

3/2/2010

Mr. Hall, R.N.
Happy Holistic Hospital
974 Serene Street
Providence, RI

Dear Mr. Hall, R.N.,

I recently completed a B.S. degree from the University of Massachusetts at Amherst, MA where I earned a G.P.A. of 3.80 in my major.

My strengths include being dedicated to the field of nursing. I am technically strong as my course records indicate and have an innate ability to communicate well with patients, co-workers, and those in authority.

I would like to meet with you to introduce myself and to learn from your experience as you were once in my position.

I have attached a resume for your review. I hope that taking time to meet with me (about ten to fifteen minutes) is acceptable to you. I admire your success in your field and am eager to learn from you.

I will contact you early next week to schedule a time for us to meet.

Sincerely,

Nancy Nunes

Enclosure: Resume

Some recent graduates may want to attempt a more direct approach. This is true cold calling. They simply pick up the telephone and start calling potential employers on their list.

Generally speaking, if you already have a connection with a person in the company or in the case of most small companies, you can just call and ask to speak to the hiring authority. If you are seeking employment in mid to large companies with layers of bureaucracy, you'll need to send an introductory letter first.

Dialing for Dollars

So, if you want to try true cold calling or what I call "Dialing for Dollars" you should read this script and practice it. Then re-write it in your own words so it comes out smooth. OK, here's the script Mary used. You can easily modify it by slightly changing the first sentence to fit your own situation.

Cold Call Script

Good morning Mr./Ms._____ My name is _____Mary_____. How are you today?

I recently completed an Associate's degree from Computational Community College in Providence, Rhode Island. I'm proud to say that my major G.P.A. was 3.75. I'm equally proud of having won a College Accounting Scholarship in 2010.

I thought that if I connected with successful people in my field that they might be able to point me in the right direction. That's why I called you.

I was hoping to meet with you for 10 or 15 minutes to introduce myself, show you my resume and get some professional advice as to where to go from here.

(Shut up and LISTEN)

Great!! What's a convenient time for you?

OK, I'll be there on _____day at ___ o'clock.

I'm looking forward to meeting with you.

You'll be surprised at how willing **most** people are to help you out. They've been there before too.

The first couple of calls will be the hardest. I suggest that you **not** call your favorite potential employer first. Make your mistakes with employers who you're not drooling over. Besides, by following this process you might be referred to that employer of your dreams by another employer. What a great inside job... being referred to the employer you want by another employer who saw potential in you. Imagine calling Ms. Sherlock at Dream Job Number One and saying "Mr. Smith was kind enough to meet with me to give me some career advice and suggested that I call you". I think you'd feel like you were on third base with no outs and Babe Ruth was at bat.

Once you get to meet with the boss, your job is to dress professionally (that's one step up from your on the job clothes), be neat and clean and be your personable inquisitive self. You want to know what the corporate or office climate is. Are there strict rules or is it an easy going atmosphere? How long do people stay at the job? What are the opportunities for advancement for someone who works here? What sets them apart from their competition?

Don't take control of the dialog unless you have to. Let them ask you questions and assist you in your search. This is how you meet the right people at the right time. As I mentioned earlier, this is how **most** jobs (estimated to be over 80%) are found...**by knowing the right person**.

Now you need to keep track of all these calls and appointments.

Interview date:_____   Telephone Number:_____

Contact person_____   Company Name:_____

Results of Contact_____

_____

_____

_____

_____

Thank you letter sent on:_____

Next follow-up date:_____

Next Follow up action_____

The Informational Interview

The informational interview is truly part of the job seeking process and is counted as part of your "day". Informational interviews generally last up to a half hour. Adding in travel time we'll call it ***an hour.***

OK, so now you have an informational interview with a boss in your chosen line of work. What should I say? What questions should I ask?

Well, to be honest with you, you should have gone on informational interviews before you even made a final decision to pursue your chosen career. I only say this so that you can correctly advise any other people who you know prior to their making a career choice.

All is not lost. You now have academic knowledge about your career choice. You may even have some form of on the job training. One thing is for sure: you are not an expert in your field. Fortunately for you, you still have a lot to learn about the ins and outs of your career as it exists in real life. This is where the informational interview after formal training comes in.

The types of questions you could ask are as follows:

How did you break into this field?

Would you recommend this field to someone like me coming up the ranks? Why or why not?

What do you like about your job?

What would you like to see changed?

What is a typical day like for you?

How has your job changed since you started?

What do you see in the future for this career?

What skills do you think will be in highest demand in the next five years?

As with any meeting, you should dress appropriately, be professional, listen more than you talk, and have good eye contact.

Before you leave the meeting be sure to ask for the name of another person in the field who might be able to give you a slightly different perspective of your chosen career. This widens your network and knowledge of the field. It is also easier than the "cold calling" you originally did to get your first interview. If Ms. Smith refers you to Mr. Jones, how hard can it be to call Mr. Jones and say that Ms. Smith was nice enough to spend some time with you and thought that he would be able to give you a different perspective? Not hard at all.

After each informational interview, send or e-mail a thank you note. Also, since your long term objective is to establish relationships with these people, contact them every month or so to keep them apprised of your progress. You never know what can happen during these follow-up phone calls. You just might get an offer you can't refuse.

Where else can I look for work?

I always recommend that you tell everyone you know that you are looking for a job. That includes former professors, family, extended family, friends, friends of extended family, etc. You get the idea. In today's high tech world it's easier than ever to get the word out. It's called "Facebook". If you don't have a Facebook account, open one. If you do have a Facebook account make sure your profile is professional looking and not full of things you don't want a prospective employer or a person referring you to an employer to see. I suggest putting your resume right up front and center (omitting any personal information like your address) with a statement about the type of work you are looking for. If you have any type of portfolio (i.e. pictures of foods you've cooked) these should be here too. Hopefully, some of your "friends" will refer you to someone with the power to interview and hire you.

You could reach out a bit and join groups or become a fan of the companies you want to work for.

Another option is "LinkedIn" which helps job seekers and employers meet through mutual acquaintances. Employers can list jobs and search for potential candidates. Job seekers can review the profile of hiring managers and discover which of their existing contacts can introduce them. You need to have a connection to use this but LinkedIn helps you do this quite easily. For more information on LinkedIn go to www.linkedin.com

The Employment Interview

You've gone on informational interviews and applied for jobs that you thought you might be qualified for. One day you get the call that an employer wants to talk with you in person. Yippee!! You got your first employment interview. I hope you are well prepared for this. All the studying and work you did, the resume writing and informational interviews you went on come down to this. This is where the rubber hits the road.

The employment interview is nothing more than a formal discussion to determine whether you and this company are a good match. It's a two way street. You need to find out if the job and the company fit you as a worker. They need to determine if you are the BEST candidate among the applicants for them and that particular job.

Not every candidate gets interviewed. Just those that seem to be a good fit, at least on paper. Once you get called in for an interview you know you made the first cut. You should feel like you're on third base with Babe Ruth at bat. You are in a very good position. There, doesn't that relieve at least some of your stress?

What do you think employers are looking for in a new hire?

They are looking for several things. First is **someone who can do the job**. You've been selected for an interview because you have the proper training for the job at hand. Now you have to convince the interviewer(s) that you are very competent in your field. Does the most competent person automatically get the job offer? Not necessarily.

Employers are also looking for someone that **fits their company structure**. They are looking for someone with whom they can get along. A lawyer I met had recently hired a new lawyer to his staff, in large part because the applicant played Foosball. (Foosball is the table soccer game played by teams of two). The applicant had put "Foosball" as an interest on his resume. It just so happened that the lawyers in that office had a Foosball game in the lunch room. They played Foosball at lunch as a team building and stress relief strategy. Since this applicant played well and fit in with the others, among other things, he was offered the job. The rationale was that all the lawyers who applied had the needed skills, but none would fit in with the group as well.

Ok, my point behind this story is that you need to let your personality shine on an interview. You can put your best foot forward by being relaxed, focused, pleasant yet professional, positive in your approach to questions, sit straight and maintain good natural eye contact. You won't get to home plate if you are self-defeating and negative during the interview.

Employers also look for **dedication** in their employees. You show them your dedication by having completed the program you studied for. You also show them dedication by having held part time jobs or internships, getting good recommendations, getting good grades and/or awards, showing that you have a good work ethic (come in early and/or stay late, stay focused, get things done on time, etc.). Remember early on when I mentioned that you had to have a real life story to back up everything on your resume? This is why. Like Ricky Ricardo used to say "You better esplain, Lucy".

Employment interviews are not casual conversations. You should do some homework. You should know something about the company that you are applying to. You should be able to answer the question, "Why do you want to work here?" A lot of information on a lot of companies is available on the Internet. Other sources of company information include newspaper articles, company sponsored advertisements, Chamber of Commerce, even employees you might know. A little research will go a long way. Who would impress you most, the candidate who knew what the company does and knows about a recent positive news story or the candidate that hadn't a clue?

You should have a response to any question that concerns your application, resume and background. I strongly suggest that you arrive to the interview about ten to fifteen minutes early. During this time you can re-read your resume so that everything is familiar to you in your short term memory. (Bring at least three copies to hand out to the interviewers). If you hadn't already completed the employment application, you will have time to complete it using your "Cheat sheet". You'll also have time to relax and compose yourself.

Interviewees are often nervous because they are afraid of what questions the interviewer will ask them. Since this interview is for your first "professional" position, there are only three things the interviewer will ask you. First, "**Tell me about yourself**", second, "**What plans do you have for your future?**" and third, "**Why should I hire you?**"

They probably won't just blurt out those questions as stated, but that's what they want to know. To answer the first question you have to be able to explain your past relevant education and work history. **It's definitely OK to brag** about any accomplishments during an interview. It's even better if your eyes light up while telling a story about your past. The second question "What plans do you have for your future?" requires more thought because you haven't lived it yet. Do you see yourself in the same job? Are you interested in pursuing more education? Do you plan on growing with the company? A note of caution here: make sure your response is work related. "Getting married and having six children" is not a good response to that question. The last question "Why should I hire you?" is the one you wanted to answer from the minute you walked in the interview room. You know who you are, you know what you are capable of and you've read the ad or job description, and researched the company so you know what they are looking for. All you need to do is explain to them that you have all the qualities and skills that they are looking for.

Homework Assignment:

Write each question on a separate piece of paper "Tell me about yourself", "What plans do you have for your future?" and "Why should I hire you?" Then answer each question in writing. Remember the three things that employers are looking for in an employee (someone who can do the job, fits their company structure, and commitment) as you carefully craft your critique of yourself.

A curveball: Some interviewers ask double edge questions like "what is your biggest weakness?" Yeah, I hate those questions too. I think the best approach is to take a weakness and make it a strength. For example you might be a bit stubborn at times but that negative trait makes you committed to getting results.

There are many more examples of possible interview questions that I believe are beyond the scope of this guide but can be accessed by searching the Internet.

One last tip. Dress at least one level up from the way you would dress on the job. If your potential job requires a business casual you should come to the interview in formal business attire. I don't suggest wearing anything less than business casual while applying for a job or going on any job interview including informational interviews.

Questions you should ask: The interview is a two way street. Usually near the end of an interview the interviewer will ask if you have any questions. You should have two to three prepared questions in addition to questions that are stimulated by information that the interviewer has shared.

You should want to know:

- What a typical day would be like if hired.
- Who you will be reporting to.
- What your hours will be.
- Whether this is the first of several interviews or if it is the first and only interview.

If this is the first and only interview, you will want to inquire about the compensation package for the position.

If more interviews will follow in the process, hold off asking the compensation question until the last interview.

When you do ask that question use the term "compensation" rather than pay. This shows the interviewer that you understand that they are offering more than just a paycheck. Benefits can include health, life, dental or other insurance, paid or unpaid vacation time, sick time, housing, parking, daycare, education, profit sharing, retirement benefits etc.

The compensation question can be asked as "What is the compensation for this position?" Then, listen attentively. Will there be potential for raises in the near future? What are the benefits that come with that job? Can they give you exact figures yet?

Specific benefits may be more important to you than straight pay. For example, you might be happier with a few less dollars in your paycheck and having free daycare where you work. The cost savings and convenience may be worth the exchange.

As to actual pay, you should know the range from your research on **O*Net OnLine** and have a general idea of what pay you are expecting but it's imperative that you hear the specifics first hand from them.

Other good sources of compensation and pay include the informational interviews you have been going to, www.salary.com, and the salary wizard at kellyservices.salary.com.

Still a bit nervous? Good. You need to practice employment interviews to be proficient at them. You wouldn't expect an up and coming actor or actress to just read their lines a few times and then go on stage without rehearsals. Neither should you attempt to "wing it" on a job interview. You shouldn't bet your vocational future on an unrehearsed self-presentation either. Look at it this way. All the work you did in school comes down to this simple "sales" meeting. Might as well package yourself in the best way you can. You are now in the business of selling your skills, personality and dedication to your first professional employer.

I suggest getting a camcorder (or cam-phone) set up facing you and having a friend role play the interviewer. Take it seriously from the first firm friendly handshake to the last. Have the interviewer ask the questions listed previously and answer them as you would on a real interview. Be sure the volume is up enough to hear when you review the clip.

When reviewing the mock interview, watch your body language for proper positioning and for nervous tics. Remember to maintain good eye contact. How clear and accurate were your answers? How was your tone? Did you seem relaxed? How did you handle asking the interviewer questions about the job? What would you do differently next time? What did your interviewer notice about your presentation? Would you have hired yourself if you were the interviewer?

This is the place to make mistakes. You can keep trying to make a good first impression on tape until you are comfortable enough for the real thing.

Researching companies and practicing employment interviews and reviewing tapes for about ***an hour and three quarters*** should get you initially prepared for your first real audition.

Thank You Notes

Whether you are coming home from an informational interview or an employment interview, you need to send them a thank you note. This is the easiest part of looking for a professional job but also the most overlooked.

All that's needed is a short note addressed to the person you met with thanking them for their time and information. Each thank you note should take **less** than *fifteen minutes* to complete.

For example after Roberto came home from an informational interview with Mr. Rotunda he wrote the following:

Roberto Perez
1098 North Street
Providence, RI 02903

3/15/2010

Mr. Robert Rotunda
Blakes Restaurant
22 Satisfaction Street
Pawtucket, RI

Dear Mr. Rotunda,

I would like to thank you for meeting with me and offering me some professional advice on how to advance in my field. I was surprised to hear how important being assertive is to move up in the cooking field. After hearing your examples and thinking about it, it makes sense to me.

I'll be sure to emphasize that aspect of my personality on future interviews.

Thank you for your time and the referral to Dino at Dino's Delicious Dining. I'll call you after I meet with him.

Sincerely,

Roberto Perez

You can see that Roberto picked up on something he learned on the informational interview and let Mr. Rotunda know that his time was well spent. He also kept the relationship growing by setting up a call back after he meets with Dino. Do you think Roberto is impressing Mr. Rotunda? You bet he is. Do you think Mr. Rotunda might talk to other people in the industry about the fine young man he met? He might.

Mary Cartier just came home from an employment interview with Mr. Numbersmith. She wrote the following thank you note:

Mary Cartier
1098 South Street
Providence, RI 02903

3/22/2010

Mr. Alfred Numbersmith
Al's Accounting
22 Count Street
Providence, RI

Dear Mr. Numbersmith,

Thank you for giving me the opportunity to discuss the Junior Accountant position you have available. I was pleased to hear that most of the duties of this position correlate highly with my academic and work experience. As we discussed, I am certain that I can maintain the pace you described with great accuracy. The opportunity to become involved in interpreting the balance sheet, profit and loss statement, and other reports to summarize current and projected company financial position truly peaks my interest in this position.

I look forward to hearing from you shortly.

Sincerely,

Mary Cartier

Similar to Roberto, Mary picked up on something she learned during the interview and let Mr. Numbersmith know that she was intelligent, still interested in the job, eager to learn, and was a classy young lady simply by sending this letter.

What an easy Day!

That's all there is to preparing for a potential job.

Writing the application took 0.5 hours.

Writing the resume took 2.5 hours.

Writing the cover letters took 0.5 hours

Finding potential employers took 0.5 hours.

Sending the cover letters and making cold calls took 1.0 hours.

Informational interview took 1.0 hours.

The research and employment interview practice took 1.75 hours.

The thank you notes took 0.25 hours.

That's it. One eight hour day to prepare yourself for the future you've been working so hard for.

Keep reading for more tips on how to get through the job hunting process.

Rejection

"I submit all my plays to the National Theatre for rejection...to assure myself I am seeing clearly" Howard Barker. (http://www.brainyquote.com),BrainyQuote.

According to Wikipedia, Howard Barker has written sixty two stage plays, eight radio plays, and thirteen television plays. "Though he is relatively unknown in his own country, Barker's works have earned him a sizable following on the European mainland where his plays get more lavish productions, and many of his plays have been translated into various languages."

It's a good thing that Mr. Barker didn't stop writing just because the National Theatre rejected his works. In fact you can see that by reading between the lines, he turns the tables on them. He makes sure his plays meet his standards by making sure the National Theatre rejects him.

Generally speaking, none of us like being rejected. Rejection brings up negative emotions such as hurt, anger, and sorrow. Rejection on an employment interview equals disappointment. This is especially true when you felt that you "Aced" the interview.

The worst part is that rejection is often a pivot point. It makes you doubt yourself a bit. Self-doubt can lead to you questioning your skills and quitting your pursuits. After all, maybe the interviewers were right not to hire you, you think.

But wait what would Mr. Barker say? He'd just laugh and move on to the next venue. He didn't let one group of critics turn him away from his goals, he pressed on and became successful (probably more successful than those National Theatre blokes).

A "do the math" reality check. How many jobs were available when you went on your last interview? Probably just one. How many applicants were there? Let's assume ten applicants. What were your chances of getting that specific job? One in ten or just 10 %. Do you think that all nine other candidates were losers? Of course not. Some including you were just as good as the one who got the position. It's a bit of a numbers game. They had to select one of the ten applicants according to their needs and preferences. Did they make the right choice? Time will tell. It couldn't hurt to hold your head up high and send them a letter wishing them well with their choice and let them know that you'd be interested in another position at their company should one become available.

Since someone else got that last job, there's now less competition in your area of expertise. Maybe it was a blessing that you didn't get that job. It could have been the job from Hell. I had one of those once. It's not fun at all.

So, try to take rejection in stride. Learn from the experience. Keep practicing your interviewing techniques and keep going on informational and employment interviews. Eventually you will find an employer smart enough to hire you.

Forms to Complete at time of hire

W-4

Once you secure that dream job in your chosen field, you'll have to complete some forms for your newest best friend, your employer. They will have you complete a W-4 form which is an IRS form that tells your employer how much Federal Income tax to withhold from your pay. The last thing you want is to owe money to the IRS next year, so it's important to get this right. The idea is to come as close to breakeven without going under. Going under means that you have to pay Uncle Sam after next April 15. Going over means that you are living on less than you actually earn while giving the Uncle an interest free loan. A little wiggle room either way is OK but try your best to hit that breakeven target. You should work with the payroll section of your new employer to help get it right.

The basic premise is that the more you claim as dependents, the more money you will receive in your paycheck. It makes sense because your tax liability at the end of the year will be lower because you will be claiming those dependents that you have to house, clothe and feed all year long. If you are single and on your own, you could claim less (i.e. 0 or 1) to break even.

Some people like to be sure they won't have an IRS problem in the future so they claim more than they have to. This allows them to have a forced savings plan just before summer vacation time when the refunds are sent out.

It's also important to note that you can change your federal withholding any time you want to change it. Suppose you pick up a part time job over and above the dream job, for example you might be hired for Christmas help. You might want to adjust the W-4 at that point then revert back to the old way after Christmas. You can access the IRS W-4 form at http://www.irs.gov/pub/irs-pdf/fw4.pdf?portlet=3

I-9 Form

The I-9 form is used to verify that each new employee is authorized to work in the United States. This is a simple form to complete but you must have the proper credentials with you. The proper credentials are listed on the following page. The free website is:

http://www.uscis.gov/files/form/i-9cnmi.pdf

E-Verify

According to Wikipedia, "E-Verify is an Internet-based, free program run by the United States Government that compares information from an employee's Employment Eligibility Verification Form I-9 to data from U.S. Government records. If the information matches, that employee is eligible to work in the United States. If there's a mismatch, E-Verify alerts the employer and the employee is allowed to work while he or she resolves the problem; they must contact the appropriate agency to resolve the mismatch within eight federal government work days from the referral date.[1] The program is operated by the Department of Homeland Security (DHS) in partnership with Social Security Administration.

According to the DHS website, more than 196,000 employers now use E-Verify. Over 1,400 companies enroll in the program every week".

Work Opportunity Tax Credit

Want to make your employer even happier that they hired you instead of someone else? Well if you fit into any of these categories you can earn a "Tax Credit" for your employer. That's money that they don't have to pay good ole Uncle Sam at tax time. If you qualify for this credit, you should build this fact into your employment interview repertoire.

So how big a deal can this be?

The Work Opportunity Tax Credit can now be as much as:

$2,400 generally for each new adult hire,

$1,200 for each summer youth hire,

$4,800 *for each new disabled veteran hire*, and

$9,000 *for each new long-term TANF recipient hired over a 2-yr. period.*

Do I qualify? You might if you fit into any of these categories:

- Hurricane Katrina employee
- Long-term family assistance recipient
- Qualified ex-felon
- Vocational rehabilitation referral
- SNAP recipient
- Unemployed veteran
- Qualified recipient of Temporary Assistance for Needy Families (TANF),
- Disconnected youth
- Qualified veteran
- Designated community resident
- Summer youth employee
- SSI recipient

Bonds 4 Jobs

Bonds 4 jobs is a Federal/Private employee bonding program which secures $5000 bonds on hard to place employees such as ex-offenders, including anyone with a record of arrest, conviction or imprisonment, and anyone who has ever been on probation or parole. Also bondable under this program are recovering substance abusers (alcohol and/or drug abuse), welfare recipients and other persons having a poor credit record or who have declared bankruptcy, economically disadvantaged youth who lack a work history, and individuals who were dishonorably discharged from the military. Others searching for work also can be classified as at-risk if the barrier to their employment can be eliminated by making them bondable.

If you fit into any of the above categories you may be bondable which means that if you steal anything from your company, embezzle, commit forgery, larceny, and are caught, the court system deals with you and your employer gets back the amount of value stolen in cash (up to $5000) from the program. The program lasts for six months.

It's a way to equalize the playing field for hard to place applicants. Hey, some of us made mistakes in our past. We don't deserve to be cast out of a chance to move on with our lives. This helps give us a fighting chance...especially with our newly developed skills. The whole process only takes one phone call and is free. Bonds4jobs can be utilized for full or part time jobs.

If you qualify for this bonding program, you should research it and work it into your employment interview.

You can learn more at www.bonds4jobs.com.

References

Dictionary of Occupational Titles http://www.occupationalinfo.org/
by the US Dept. of Labor.

O*NET OnLine is created for the U.S. Department of Labor,
Employment & Training Administration (http://www.doleta.gov/),
by the National Center for O*NET Development.

The Job Hunting Handbook; published by the Dahlstrom & Company

Mapquest www.mapquest.com

Wikipedia® is a registered trademark of the Wikimedia Foundation, Inc., a non-profit organization.
www.wikipedia.org
(http://www.brainyquote.com),BrainyQuote.

www.bonds4jobs.com.

www.doleta.gov/business/incentives/opptax, Work Opportunity Tax Credit

http://www.irs.gov/pub/irs-pdf/fw4.pdf?portlet=3, W-4 Form

http://www.uscis.gov/files/form/i-9_cnmi.pdf, I-9 Form

About the Author

Andre Mayer graduated from Providence College with a major in Psychology and then received a graduate degree in Counseling from the University of Rhode Island. He then pursued the equivalent of a Bachelor's degree in Business from Bryant College.

Upon graduation from URI, Mr. Mayer worked as a Job Seeking Skills Instructor at a community action program. He then went on to work for twenty eight years for the State Vocational Rehabilitation Agency in Rhode Island. There Mr. Mayer was responsible for assisting people with disabilities of all kinds to obtain and maintain employment. He worked with high school students, college students, and the general adult populations.

Eager to help more people, Mr. Mayer started his own private Rehabilitation Company, Quality Rehabilitation Services which specialized in helping injured workers to return to work.

Other positions which Mr. Mayer held include Chief Business Enterprises Supervisor at the State of R.I., Services for the Blind, Adjunct Professor at the Community College of Rhode Island, Mental Health Counselor at Counseling and Intervention Services and Recruiter and Placement Specialist at the Cookie Place Culinary Arts School.

You can contact Mr. Mayer at agmaye@gmail.com